PUPPIES

Sandie Lee Books

Puppies

You have probably seen a puppy or two before. You may have even had your own puppy at one time. Puppies are really cute and fun to play with, but like all baby animals, they have special needs. Some puppies are born really small and others are already quite large. In this article we are going to explore all things puppy. You might even discover some new facts and fun ideas. So let's get started.

Newborn Puppies

Did you know there is around 400 different breeds of puppies and they all started out as a newborn? Puppies can be born any time of the year. Newborn puppies are born blind and helpless, with very little fur. They must be kept warm and dry. Puppies depend on their moms for everything at this stage of their lives.

Finding Mom

Did you know newborn puppies have a great sense of smell? Even though newborn puppies are born blind and deaf, they can use their powerful sniffers. Puppies can smell and feel their way around their bedding area to find mom. This helps them locate their mother when it is time to eat.

What Puppies Eat

Did you know puppies nurse milk from their mother? She can feed several puppies at one time. In fact, some female dogs can have up to 10 puppies in a single litter. The milk mom supply is full of nutrients to help her puppies grow. Once a puppy reaches around 4 weeks old, it can start to eat soft dog food.

How Long With Mom?

Did you know puppies can leave their mother as young as 5 weeks old, but it is not a wise idea? Most puppies do better when left with their mother for at least 8 weeks. During this time, the mother dog will teach her puppies basic skills and help them to become socialized.

How Long With Mom?

Did you know puppies can communicate? Puppies will let their mother know when they are hungry, cold or upset. They do this by making a whining sound. As the puppy becomes older, it will use soft growling and grunting noises to let mom know it needs her. Soon after it will try to bark.

Getting Teeth

Did you know puppies are born without teeth? They start to grow teeth through the first few weeks of their lives. They get 28 teeth in total. When a puppy is 'teething' or getting new teeth, it will like to chew on things. It will chew on different textures to help relieve the pain.

Sleeping Puppy

Did you know that puppies sleep most of the time? This is because puppies use sleep to restore their bodies and to grow. Young puppies may only be awake for minutes at a time. As the puppy gets older it will have the ability to stay awake and be alert for longer periods of time.

Playing Puppy

Did you know puppies learn a lot through playing? Very young puppies must first learn to walk. They do this by pulling themselves along the floor on their bellies. Soon after, the puppy will learn to run and chase after toys and their littermates. Some puppies will wrestle and jump while playing together.

Learning to Bark

Did you know that all puppies bark, some more than others? Puppies must find their bark. They do this by practicing when they are very young. It may take some time before a puppy's bark sounds normal. It will start out with squeaks, whines and crying noises. Usually by 10 weeks old a puppy is close to having a bark.

Learning New Skills

Did you know some puppies have jobs? Dogs like German Shepherds are used in the police force, while Beagles make good hunting dogs. If a dog has a job to do, it starts its training as a puppy. This is so the puppy will grow up learning the skills it will need to have as an adult.

Learning to Swim

Did you know most puppies are natural swimmers? Unlike you and me, puppies do not need to learn how to swim. When you put a puppy into water, you will notice its legs immediately start to move. This form of swimming is called, the 'doggy paddle.' Some breeds of dog, like Spaniels, love being in the water.

The Chihuahua

Out of all the puppy breeds, the chihuahua is the smallest. This little dog is born weighing only about 3 to 4 ounces. These puppies are very delicate and need lots of care and attention. It is important to keep them warm and safe from falls or from being accidentally stepped on.

The Great Dane

Great Danes are one of the largest dog breeds in the world. Newborn great dane puppies can weigh anywhere from 1 to 2 pounds. They may be born bigger and with longer legs, but they are still helpless. Like all newborns, the great dane puppy will need its mom for care, food and warmth.

The Bulldog

Bulldog puppies are born stocky, with wide shoulders and big round heads. Most female bulldogs will only give birth to one or two puppies at a time. This is because the bulldog puppy's head is very large and round. This makes it difficult for the bulldog female to give birth to more than a couple of puppies at a time.

Quiz

Question 1: How many breeds of puppies are there in the world today?

Answer 1: There are around 400 different puppy breeds

Question 2: At what age does a puppy first sample soft dog food?

Answer 2: 4 weeks of age

Question 3: How many teeth do puppies have?

Answer 3: They have 28 teeth

Question 4: What technique does a puppy use when it is swimming? Hint; it's the same as humans

Answer 4: The doggy paddle

Question 5: Which breed of dog is the tallest?

Answer 5: The great dane

Thank you for checking out another addition from Sandie Lee Books! Make sure to check out Amazon.com for many other great titles.